1/20/19

Anchored!

To: Andrew & family

Trust God and trust the process! Write the Vision and make it plain!

Be Blessed!

beblesseddaily.com

Anchored!

Be Blessed!
Daily Collection
Volume 1

Adelai Brown

ISBN-13: 9781517524210
ISBN-10: 1517524210
Library of Congress Control Number: 2015916046
CreateSpace Independent Publishing Platform
North Charleston, South Carolina

Introduction

*Lord, to whom shall we go? You
have the words of eternal life.*

John 6:68 (NKJV)

Life has a tendency to beat against one's will
to stay afloat. There are many circumstances
on the voyage of life that can cause mental,
physical, and spiritual capsizing. As defined in
Merriam-Webster Unabridged, "An anchor is a
heavy device that is attached to a boat or ship
by a rope or chain and that is thrown into the
water to hold the boat or ship in place; it is also
a person or thing that provides strength and
support." *Anchored!* was written to assist read-
ers in the prevention of emotional and spiritual

drifting and drowning. Storms are inevitable, but being anchored keeps one in place. Read an "anchor" daily or as often as you need. Use the weight of the messages to help hold your being in position. Ideas that I've encountered along the way, life experiences, and people are what inspired these daily anchors. They all end with the phrase "Be Blessed!" because I want you to know that every anchor bids you blessings as you read. My intention is that as you read, you will receive strength, stability, and support to encourage healthy living

Day 1

Happy New Year's and best wishes to you this year. Make this a year of no regrets. Pull away from your usual routine - chart new paths and conquer new territories. What you invest in yourself will be rewarded with great returns. Be Blessed!

Day 2

Never allow your selfish ambitions to make you insensitive to your surroundings. The pursuit of happiness can be your downfall if you're not careful. Keep your beloved in mind. Only seek what truly matters.
Be Blessed!

Day 3

Expectations don't guarantee substance. You must take responsibility for your own actions, and make the most of what you have. Don't complain about anything that you're not willing to change. Hard work and patience are vital keys to success.

Be Blessed!

Day 4

Your identity isn't validated by your titles, cars, or homes. The substance you have within makes you who you are. Being your authentic self is a necessity. Seek your manufacturer for directions on how to use your software.
Be Blessed!

Day 5

Give your burdens to the One who is
equipped to handle all complications. There
is an infinite source of provision awaiting you
to receive. If someone or something is worth
fighting for, do your best, and have faith.
Be Blessed!

Day 6

When life beats you down, allow faith to lift you up. Joy is not a mood to fall in and out of; it is a state of being. Optimism opens doors. Is your glass half-empty or half-full?
Be Blessed!

Day 7

Let go, and let God. Don't allow life's problems to spiral out of control. Honestly address them as they arise, and be willing to make necessary changes. The storms of life don't discriminate. Stay anchored.
Be Blessed!

Day 8

Live a purposeful life that brings the best
out of you. Don't do the same things while
expecting a different result. Time waits
on no one.
Be Blessed!

Day 9

If you've ever questioned your existence, know
that *you* were created for a purpose. Seek your
source for substance. Tests make you wiser
and stronger. Love yourself enough to try.
Be Blessed!

Day 10

Your money is spent where your heart is.
Material things can't take the place of time
and affection. You should matter more to
others than what you do for them.
Communicate with those you love.
Be Blessed!

Day 11

Do you think you're giving life your best, or are you doing just enough to get by? Never envy others for completing the work you didn't finish. You must be accountable.
Be Blessed!

Day 12

Don't take for granted the love you have. You never know when it may be gone. Swallow your pride, and do what it takes. You don't miss what you have until it's gone.
Be Blessed!

Day 13

Today may be a good day or maybe not.
Nevertheless, today is a day that you've been
blessed with. Make the most of *every* minute
that you have. The more you believe in
yourself, the further along you'll be.
Be Blessed!

Day 14

The different areas of your life are intertwined. Choices made during leisure time affect personal and professional relationships. Think first - respond versus reacting.
Be Blessed!

Day 15

Look into the mirror. Do you like what you see? Clothes, shoes, makeup, and hair can't mask who you are at the core. Beauty comes from within. No one can hide true ugliness.
Be Blessed!

Day 16

When you know what you're doing is wrong, repetition becomes dangerous. Discipline and condition yourself for greatness. In the end, more is gained by doing what is right.
Be Blessed!

Day 17

Who you are can't be found in a magazine or seen through the television. Search from within. When faced with questions about creation, seek the Creator.

Be Blessed!

Day 18

An unsuccessful attempt isn't a failed attempt unless it's your last attempt. Use the knowledge you gain through unfavorable circumstances, and improvise. Victory is yours as long as you believe it.
Be Blessed!

Day 19

Your eyes and ears are the entrances to your heart. Watch and listen to things that enhance your character and don't cloud your judgment. Make real efforts to live on purpose.
Be Blessed!

Day 20

Choosing to stay a situation that limits self-expression is actually a sign of settling for less. Opinions come in like a hurricane, so you must be able to weather the storm. In order to recognize and appreciate joy, you must be aware of what pain is.

Be Blessed!

Day 21

You can get an E for effort but why not get an
A for achievement? Life is what you make of
it. Don't waste time feeling sorry for yourself.
Take advantage of the privileges and resources
you have. Many died for your right to live.
Be Blessed!

Day 22

Tests and trials are alerts to blessings that are already en route to you. Hold on, and have *faith* until the storm blows over. Trouble doesn't last always.
Be Blessed!

Day 23

Confidence is the key to success. It's not what you do; instead, it's what you believe that you can do. Did you know that you were created with a purpose? The lessons you learn from your mistakes will lead you to your success.

Be Blessed!

Day 24

Challenges allow you to see how strong you truly are. Never run from adversity; instead, face it with boldness and confidence. In Christ all things are possible.

Be Blessed!

Day 25

Life has twists and turns and mountains and valleys, but we must hold on to the harness of God's promises to stay on track. Get to know your Father in heaven. He will protect and guide you to places you've never imagined.
Just believe, and take that first step.
Be Blessed!

Day 26

Don't just talk about your dreams; be about your dreams coming true. Actions speak louder than words. Start doing what you've been talking and dreaming about. The greatest failure is to never try at all. Be Blessed!

Day 27

Your situation is never as bad as it seems.
There will always be times in life that changes
must be made. There are a lot of opportunities
in this world for you to take advantage of.
Make the most out of your days, and live a
more fulfilling life!
Be Blessed!

Day 28

Love makes life worth living. Love is gentle, peaceful, and forgiving. God is love, and remember this: if no one else in this world loves you, He does, and He wants the best for you.
Be Blessed!

Day 29

The expectations of others often cause interference with one's purpose. God had a unique assignment in mind when he created you. Realize your importance, and follow His lead.
Be Blessed!

Day 30

There's more to life than reaching the top.
The side of the mountain is where you grow
and take root to become the person you aspire
to be. The top can be lonely, but the journey
up will prepare you for the destination.
Be Blessed!

Day 31

Let go, and let God. Worrying about a problem will never bring about a resolution. Do the best you can to make your situation pleasant. You can only control your actions.
Don't compare yourself to others.
Be Blessed!

Day 32

It's time to leave your past behind so that you can move forward. Life is a continuous cycle of change. Being exposed to new things will force you to grow. Focus your thoughts, and your footsteps will follow. Walk into your season.

Be Blessed!

Day 33

Be creative, and try something that's different
or new to you. God blessed this land with
diversity so that we would always have places
to go and people to meet. You are constantly
changing—whether you like it or not. Let
your mind grow, and be renewed.
Be Blessed!

Day 34

Avoid unnecessary confrontation whenever possible. You don't always have to voice your opinion or make a scene to get your point across. Silence often speaks very loud. We are all different, so unique points of view are inevitable. Respect others, and respect shall be received in return.

Be Blessed!

Day 35

Hold on. Times will get hard, and situations may seem unbearable. The name of the Lord is strong; He is a mighty tower. Seek Him for help, and He will deliver you from your dilemmas. Stop trying to do it all alone.
God loves you, and so do I.
Be Blessed!

Day 36

Many times our shortcuts lead us into the traffic jams of life. There will not always be a shorter route or an easier way to get the job done. You must roll up your sleeves and put the hard work in. You're headed in the right direction once you allow Jesus to drive.

Be Blessed!

Day 37

Jesus will never reject you. He has open arm, and He is waiting for you to run to Him. Don't let what you're currently doing hinder you from inhabiting a better future. He will dry your tears and turn your darkness into the brightest light. Give yourself another chance. Jesus already has.
Be Blessed!

Day 38

No matter what you go through or what trouble comes your way, God is always in control. There is no problem too big or too small for Him to handle. Trust Him, and He will set you free from misery and delusions of defeat.

Be Blessed!

Day 39

This is your day, so claim it as such. Live your life expecting greatness. Don't allow negative thoughts and people to control your personal well-being. Make decisions that compliment your purpose.

Be Blessed!

Day 40

There are many things in life that you may never understand. When pursuing the unknown, allow God to answer your questions and give you peace and courage. Persistence renders failure powerless.
Be Blessed!

Day 41

Let life be the game that you always wanted to play. Set your imagination free, and your dreams will become a reality. You can be your own adversary or ally. Give your best in all that you do.
Be Blessed!

Day 42

Work hard, and be enthusiastic about what you're doing. Tasks may get difficult, but remember that you are working toward fulfilling your unique purpose. Take pride in what you do.
Be Blessed!

Day 43

Put your best foot forward, and take that step.
You will never know what life has in store
for you if you never step out of your comfort
zone. Trust in Jesus, and allow Him to guide
you through life. You deserve to and must live
life to its maximum potential.
Be Blessed!

Day 44

Your life is what you make it. You get back whatever you invest in yourself. . Love yourself and believe you can do anything you put your mind to. Make a decision.
Be Blessed!

Day 45

Finish what you've started. Many people know how to start projects but lack the skills needed to finish. Pace yourself, and take pride in what you're doing. If you're not pleased with your current situation, redirect your focus.
Be Blessed!

Day 46

Take inventory of your life, and figure out
exactly where you are. You must determine
what you need to keep and what you need to
do away with. How will you move ahead if
you're not clear on where you're
currently located?
Be Blessed!

Day 47

Be thankful for all blessings—both big and small. Don't take the little things for granted. Your well may run dry unexpectedly. Be appreciative in all things.
Be Blessed!

Day 48

The time is now. Stop doing the same things while expecting different results. Give your life a makeover. Go to new places, and meet new people. You will not see change if actions remain the same. Care about yourself before you expect others to care for you.

Be Blessed!

Day 49

Keep your eyes on the prize. There will be many distractions and pit stops in life. You must remain focused. God created you to be extraordinary. Maximize your potential.
Be Blessed!

Day 50

Life is like riding a roller coaster. There are exciting inclines and scary drops and falls, and that uncertainty is all a part of the ride. Figure out what you want out of life, and put it on paper. If you can see your dream, then you can achieve it. Life gives you back what you put into it. Be Blessed!

Day 51

Many people want something for nothing. You will reap what you sow in life. Stop complaining, and stop putting yourself down! God loves you and wants the best for you. The question is this: Do you want the best for yourself? Be Blessed!

Day 52

You may have lost a loved one, but his or
her memory lives on with you. No one lives
forever. There are many things in life that we
won't ever understand. Thank God for the
time you shared, and pray that you meet again
in heaven.
Be Blessed!

Day 53

Be mindful of the company you keep. Many may claim to be supportive, but they only want to witness your demise. You can't tell everyone your dreams, but your secrets are safe with Jesus. Try something new. Love yourself enough not to deal with foolishness.
Be Blessed!

Day 54

To have a great day is a choice you must make daily. It's your season for breakthrough and overflow. Open your mind to receive whatever is necessary for you to fulfill your purpose
Be Blessed!

Day 55

Life may knock you down like the waves
of the sea, but that's not a reason for you to
drown. Don't find comfort in your pain.
Make the most out of every situation.
Be Blessed!

Day 56

You should not believe everything you hear.
You must research the information that's given
to you before you assume that it's correct.
There are always wolves in sheep's clothing
that are ready to steal your peace and joy. The
flock you associate with may be
predators in disguise.
Be Blessed!

Day 57

Never let the way others live keep you from getting to know Jesus. He loves you unconditionally and wants the best for you. Everything can't be explained. If you've ever felt alone, empty, confused, and fed up, Jesus is the answer to your questions.

Be Blessed!

Day 58

You can't let anyone or anything get between you and your destiny. Surround yourself with people who challenge and encourage you to do better. If you are the sharpest knife in your drawer of friends, you should familiarize yourself with more insightful surroundings.
Be Blessed!

Day 59

Being unsuccessful or unhappy is not an option. Do not let your comfort zone become a stumbling block along the road of life. You will never know what you can do until you get out and challenge yourself. With Jesus, all possibilities are promising.

Be Blessed!

Day 60

It doesn't matter how you feel about yourself:
God still loves you unconditionally. Keep your
head up, and try to always find the purpose of
every situation in life. What doesn't kill you
will make you stronger.
Be Blessed!

Day 61

Push yourself to the limit every time. Your goals are as unique as your fingerprint. Invest your time and energy into living a more fulfilling life. Your success and happiness are what you make of them.

Be Blessed!

Day 62

Be bold in the Lord, and never be afraid to
stand up for what you believe in. We must
pursue life with determination and respect.
Never take for granted the blessings you have.
You never miss the water until your
well runs dry.
Be Blessed!

Day 63

Live life to the fullest. There is enough opportunity in this world for everyone to succeed. Don't step on the toes of others; instead, help each other rise to the top. Surround yourself with positive people. There is strength in numbers.
Be Blessed!

Day 64

Love is greater than any adversity you will ever face. There's a lot more to life than the clothes you wear and the car you drive. There are unique capabilities that only you possess. The world needs you to make it a better place.
Be Blessed!

Day 65

Seek God first. His wisdom, love, and peace will overcome your atmosphere. People who hold grudges allow others to control their livelihood. Trust in your Creator.
Be Blessed!

Day 66

Establish goals and boundaries for your future. Settling is not an option. Stand up for what you believe in. Anything worth having is worth fighting for. Remain faithful, and embrace the idea that trouble doesn't last forever!
Be Blessed!

Day 67

Align your priorities and handle your business before you render judgment about what takes place in the homes of others. Comparison is a form of insecurity. Everyone has problems that only Jesus can solve. Be mindful of throwing stones when we all live in glass homes.
Be Blessed!

Day 68

Those who are well educated and highly skilled aren't always the most successful. Apply your best effort to everything you do. Pay attention when considering others.
Be Blessed!

Day 69

Let it go. Stop trying to make something out
of nothing. Making "safe" decisions can prove
to be damaging later. Life is too short. Invest
your time in interests of substance. Things in
your life will only get better if you take the
necessary steps to implement change. God
created us to live in abundance, but are you?
Be Blessed!

Day 70

Don't allow your pride to cause destiny to slip through your fingers. No one is perfect, and we all need help from others. Life is tough, but when you surround yourself with the right people and places, you will flourish and grow. Be Blessed!

Day 71

Stay anchored, no matter how strong the waves of life may get. You can do more than you could ever ask, think, or hope with the power of Christ within you. Allow Him into your heart. Change consists of cycles. Let this cycle of your life be built on the solid Rock. Be Blessed!

Day 72

You are the company you keep. Don't sit
in the company of those who don't want to
succeed. They are parasites that will suck the
life out of you. Focus on things that are pure,
peaceful, and inspiring. You can't always
let the left hand know what the right
hand is doing.
Be Blessed!

Day 73

There may be situations in your life that seem too great for you to handle. Trust, believe, and give your burdens to Jesus. He doesn't penalize your for your past; He wants you to walk into a future of peace. Stop fighting battles that aren't yours.
Be Blessed!

Day 74

Life is lovely, and the world is your playground. Do you want to come out and play? Living out of the box minimizes boundaries. If you do not come out and play, you will miss out on the sunshine of living. Be Blessed!

Day 75

You truly reap what you sow. Please believe that when you make a decision—whether it is conscious or not—it has an effect on you, whether positive or negative. Always think first. Remember that the blame doesn't always fall on someone else.

Be Blessed!

Day 76

Why would one allow ignorant people to bother them when being ignorant is in their nature? Only God can change the hearts of men. Know your place in their process of fulfilling their purpose.
Be Blessed!

Day 77

Obstacles are a part of everyday life. Understand that there is a lesson learned with every dilemma encountered. Pressure turns coal into beautiful diamonds. Don't buckle under pressure ; instead, rise to the occasion. Be Blessed!

Day 78

Remember that every season has a reason. Love without limitations, and be loved without limitations. Don't jeopardize solid relationship for those who are not sincere. The greener grass on the other side of the fence may be an illusion.
Be Blessed!

Day 79

In all things, give thanks. Your situation may be bad, but it could be worse. Gratitude opens the door for prosperity. Trust the journey to lead you to your intended destination.
Be Blessed!

Day 80

Your life is what you make of it. Don't expect others to cater to you by reading your mind. Never let people tell you what you want to hear; instead, listen to what you need to hear. You can't clean someone's house if your home is spiritually filthy. Practice what you preach, or don't preach at all.
Be Blessed!

Day 81

You can't ever truly love someone until you love yourself. You can't truly love yourself until you love God and receive the love He has for you. Let go of your hurt and pain to make room for the healing that awaits you.
Be Blessed!

Day 82

When you've made up your mind to step out on faith, *do not turn back*. There will be many pitfalls, but remember that God is always in control. He uses the tough times in life to show you how strong He truly is. Trust your Creator. Be Blessed!

Day 83

Question your position and your reasons for being where you are. Do you strive to please others, or are you following your heart? Your life is what you make of it. You can't blame anyone for your shortcomings.
Be Blessed!

Day 84

What are you doing right now? Are you living life expecting things to get better, or are you waiting for things to fail? Don't wait for tomorrow because tomorrow may never come knocking on your door. Maximize every moment..
Be Blessed!

Day 85

You are a role model, whether you like it or not. It's not about you; it's about the people who are watching you and wanting to do the things you're doing. Take the route of integrity that allows you to live at your maximum potential.

Be Blessed!

Day 86

You were created to do great things during your stay on this planet. Stop worrying about what the person next to you is doing, unless you're working with them. Jealousy is consuming. Comparison robs one of joy. God has a unique blessing with your name on it.
Be Blessed!

Day 87

God puts people in your life for a reason.
Obedience is required even if you don't
understand. Ask God for the faith you need
to make all your dreams come true, and
they will come true.
Be Blessed!

Day 88

Things aren't always the way they seem.
Take time to evaluate the situation and view
all sides of the story. Assumptions aren't
always accurate.
Be Blessed!

Day 89

Actions speak louder than words. Don't just tell others what to do. Show them how it's done. Never expect from others that which you're not willing to do yourself.
Be Blessed!

Day 90

When faced with difficult decisions, *make a move*. How will you know if you're going in the right direction if you're stagnant? Make adjustments when needed.

Be Blessed!

Day 91

Happiness doesn't always knock on your door; you must make it happen. Don't expect others to make you feel complete. If you do, you will always be broken.

Be Blessed!

Day 92

The decisions you make now will affect you and those around you for years to come. Never allow selfish motives to cloud your judgment. Honesty is the key.
Be Blessed!

Day 93

Swallow your pride, and do what needs to be done. Forget about what others think because only you can walk in your shoes. Trying to walk in the shoes of others is like having two left feet.
Be Blessed!

Day 94

Tests and trials come to make you stronger.
Buckling under pressure is a sign of weakness.
Pressure separates the real from the fake. Your
purpose is a treasure.
Be Blessed!

Day 95

First things first: many external circumstances arise from internal issues and aren't acknowledged or properly dealt with. Be honest with yourself about yourself.
Be Blessed!

Day 96

Give to others, as you would like to receive.
A closed hand can't be a blessing, nor can it
accept blessings. One thing holds true: what
goes around comes around.
Be Blessed!

Day 97

Let your faith bring you gifts that money can't buy and take you places that transportation can't reach. A poor person is one who allows memories to cloud and overcast their purpose. Position yourself for the future. Know the place of your past.

Be Blessed!

Day 98

When burdens get too heavy to carry, it's
not about trying harder. It's about
surrendering to the One who has the answer.
Prayer changes things.
Be Blessed!

Day 99

Strength is a trait we like to portray, but
we often feel very inadequate on the inside.
Understand your place, and in your weakness,
you will be made strong. There is
power in vulnerability.
Be Blessed!

Day 100

Make the most of your interactions with others. You'll never know when it's your last time. Try to see the good in others because you never know who you may be entertaining. Be Blessed!

Day 101

Give credit where credit is due. Only those who are insecure have trouble giving compliments to others. There is enough wealth in this world for everyone to succeed. Be Blessed!

Day 102

People who are hurting often hurt other people. Be mindful of how you treat others. The hand that causes pain will receive it *in return*. Don't allow a false sense of pride to cloud your judgment.
Be Blessed!

Day 103

Right is right, and wrong is wrong. You can justify your actions, but that doesn't make them right. When others hurt you, it's a tough pill to swallow. Be mindful that you're not writing your own prescriptions.
Be Blessed!

Day 104

Don't make excuses—they're just crutches to lean on. Admit your mistakes, and do better the next time. No need to cry over spilled milk. Have a prosperous day.
Be Blessed!

Day 105

The more you get to know God, the more
you get to know yourself. Your potential is
limitless. Have faith and confidence in the
God in you to expose you to a
glorious existence.
Be Blessed!

Day 106

Never get upset with anyone for not doing something for you that you can do for yourself. Take control of your life. Keep your eyes on the prize. The best is yet to come. Be Blessed!

Day 107

The biggest problem you will face in life is limiting yourself. The sky is the limit, but without belief your dreams can't come true. You are your greatest critic. Don't surrender before you go to battle.

Be Blessed!

Day 108

Jealousy leads to defeat. Don't envy others; just work harder to obtain your goals. No two people were meant to be the same. Embrace your individuality.
Be Blessed!

Day 109

You have a lot to be thankful for. Don't live in the past. If it didn't kill you, it made you stronger. Jesus is all you need.
Be Blessed!

Day 110

If you keep experiencing the same problems with different people, then you may be the one with issues. Take time to look in the mirror and address your flaws. Embrace constructive criticism.
Be Blessed!

Day 111

This is it. Leave your negative thoughts and
actions behind as you move forward. Open
your mind, and allow yourself to have a vision.
Live to your maximum potential.
Be Blessed!

Day 112

Every day is a chance to start a new year.
Embrace your essence and live on purpose.
You are not what you've done.
Be Blessed!

Day 113

You can change many things about yourself, but you can't change your past. Accept who you've become, and strive to do better. Make the most of every opportunity.

Be Blessed!

Day 114

Never give up. Shortcuts aren't always the best
way to go. Tests increase your stamina and
build character. Surround yourself
with a positive atmosphere that brings out
the best in you.
Be Blessed!

$\mathcal{D}ay$ *115*

Dreams and ambitions are the vehicles you need in order to live a fulfilling life. Fuel these vehicles with optimism and positive surroundings so that they can get you where you're trying to go. You should never be afraid of change; instead, your fear should be of staying the same.
Be Blessed!

Day 116

Do whatever it takes. Don't settle for being average. Push yourself to excel far above the limits of mediocrity. You aren't supposed to be like everyone else.
Be Blessed!

Day 117

Walk a straight line. It's the fastest way to get where you're going. Don't let life's twists and turns get you off track. God has a course that's perfect for you.
Be Blessed!

Day 118

Your pain is an indication of your prosperity.
Don't let negativity trick you into doubting
yourself. Stay the course of life. Your rewards
are inevitable.
Be Blessed!

Day 119

Don't procrastinate. Time waits for no one. Love life, and step out on faith. Knock on every door until your door opens. The only way to fail is by giving up. Stand strong. Be Blessed!

Day 120

At some point in your life, you will come to
see that many people in this world have it
worse than you. Rejoice in your hard times.
They will make your good times greater.
Troubles won't always last.
Be Blessed!

Day 121

Interact with others in a way that mirrors
how you want them to respond to you. Never
look down on anyone. Be a blessing
by blessing others.
Be Blessed!

Day 122

Family is priceless. Don't forsake the power of connection. Embrace the similarities and differences of others. There is strength in connections.
Be Blessed!

Day 123

Every great journey must start with a little step. You won't have all of the directions, so faith must be your map. God is the ultimate GPS system.
Be Blessed!

Day 124

When you have hate in your heart or hold grudges, you only hurt yourself. How can you expect God to forgive you for your sins when you won't forgive others for what they've done to you? Remember that you will reap what you sow.
Be Blessed!

Day 125

It's not all about you. Put purpose first, and God will put you first. When you close your hands, nothing can go out, nor can anything come in. Being a blessing is always in season. Be Blessed!

Day 126

What road are you traveling on? Remember that the easy way isn't always the best way. Short cuts often come with long term consequences.
Be Blessed!

Day 127

Keep your head up through the rough times,
for you must always keep your eyes on the
prize. Don't have a pity party because you're
the only person who will attend. Have faith,
and wait on the Lord. He always holds up His
end of the deal—will you?
Be Blessed!

Day 128

This is your day. Step into your season. God created us all to be unique, so why are so many of us trying to be someone else? You must find your purpose through your identity. Get comfortable in your skin; you're stuck in it anyway.
Be Blessed!

Day 129

When you know where you have come from, you will have a better idea of where you're going. Insanity is doing the same thing over and over while expecting a different result. If you want change, you must make accommodations for change.

Be Blessed!

Day 130

Anyone that would rather settle with just getting by or being like everyone else doesn't have much love for himself or herself. The sky is the limit. Don't allow yourself to stay in the bucket with crabs. What you sacrifice can't compare to what you will gain.

Be Blessed!

Day 131

If you build a house without a foundation,
it is sure to fall. You can't help others when
you're standing in sinking sand. Get yourself
together first. Stability allows you not to fall
when leaning down to help others up.
Jesus is your solid rock.
Be Blessed!

Day 132

When you figure out what's different about you, you will find your purpose in life. The more you get to know God, the more you will get to know yourself.
Be Blessed!

Day 133

Let it go. Instead of focusing on what you've lost, focus on what you have left. Change what you can, and leave the rest to God. It isn't your battle to fight.
Be Blessed!

Day 134

The wise are hungry for the truth, while fools feed on the trash. Never live in denial. Surround yourself with positive people who will tell you what you need to hear, not what you want to hear. You roll the dice, but God determines how they fall.
Be Blessed!

Day 135

Anything you want can be yours if you have faith and work hard. Grudges are roadblocks used to hinder your blessings. How can you expect God to forgive and bless you when you won't forgive others? Release negative energy for positive gains.

Be Blessed!

Day 136

This is your day. Reach for the stars in the time that you have. Tomorrow is a dangerous word because it never comes for many. Do what you can right now. You never know whether today will be your last tomorrow. Be Blessed!

Day 137

Your brightest days come after your darkest hours. Have faith, and continue to push yourself. You must do what you have never done to get what you've never had.
Be Blessed!

Day 138

Never give up. You must do whatever it takes to make your dreams come true. Life isn't easy, and nothing is fair, but you must keep pushing on. You are here for a reason. Seek your purpose, and humble yourself.
Wisdom conquers adversity.
Be Blessed!

Day 139

Never forget where you came from. The same people you meet on the way up will be there on your way down. Never judge others because you will be judged by the same standards. No one is better than you; people are just different.

Be Blessed!

Day 140

What you do today sets the tone for the rest of the year. Live every day as if it's your last. Make the most of your life while you can. This is your best year yet.
Be Blessed!

Day 141

Is what people think of you more important than what you think of yourself? When the focus is only external, it makes room for internal deterioration. Who wants a pretty box wrapped up with no gift inside? Your substance is more important than
your appearance.
Be Blessed!

Day 142

Don't get weary when others do you wrong because God never sleeps. Treat others how you want to be treated, not how they treat you. You can't reap a good harvest if you are planting bad seeds.

Be Blessed!

Day 143

Don't be quick to pass judgment on your peers. You never know who God is or whose eyes He's looking at you through. Go out of your way to bless others because God will bless you in return.

Be Blessed!

Day 144

Victory is yours if you want it. Do you? Never let people and circumstances get in the way of your destiny. Gold must be put through the fire to reach its true beauty and purity. You are worth more than silver or gold. The only way to lose is to give up.

Be Blessed!

Day 145

You can have all the riches of this world, but if you're not happy with yourself, what good will they do? Focus on becoming better from the inside, and your beauty will glow on the outside.
Be Blessed!

Day 146

It's better to give than to receive. The more you give, the more God will supply you with your heart's desires. Never do things just for the public to see. Be a blessing when only God is looking. Everyone needs a shoulder to lean on.
Be Blessed!

Day 147

You must have honest and realistic expectations for yourself and others. Many people are quick to point out the faults of others while avoiding the skeletons in their own closets. Remember that you will be judged by the same standard with which you judge others. Improve to pay it forward.
Be Blessed!

Day 148

Do something out of the ordinary. Add substance to your life by doing unique things that complement your personality. Challenge yourself to live a more fulfilling life.
Be Blessed!

Day 149

There are things in life that are never spoken
of due to the hurt and shame they expose.
Pain is a part of the healing process. Confront
your weaknesses head on, and then you will
see how strong you really are. Knowing who
you are and being completely comfortable
with that person brings true peace.
Be Blessed!

Day 150

You will be held accountable for the decisions
you choose to make in life. Living with a chip
on your shoulder could be your demise. You
get back what you give, and bad things do
happen to good people. If you want a position,
you must first position yourself to attain it.
Be optimistic, and stop having a pity party. It
only wastes time and energy.
Be Blessed!

Day 151

You are the company you keep. You can't surround yourself with negative people and expect positive outcomes. Value your time, and spend it wisely. Invest more time in talking to God and allowing Him to be your best audience.

Be Blessed!

Day 152

Keep your eyes on the prize. God's plan for you is greater than any plan you could ever imagine. Focus on your inner beauty, and your outer beauty will begin to shine.
Be Blessed!

Day 153

God desires for us to love Him with a clean heart. Let go of all the malice in your life. Negative thoughts are standing between you and your destiny. Focus on being closer to Jesus, and your dreams will come true.
Be Blessed!

Day 154

Think before you speak. Sometimes it's not what you say but how you say it. Talk *to* people, not *at* them. You must give respect in order to receive it.
Be Blessed!

Day 155

Take the first step. You don't have to see the whole journey. Just start moving your feet. With each step, you're getting closer to your destiny. Jesus is always with you, especially when you're tired and weary.

Be Blessed!

Day 156

You can always make things better in your life by helping others. God blesses those who are a blessing. When your hands are closed, nothing goes out, but nothing can come in.
Be Blessed!

Day 157

Every great journey starts with the first step.
You won't have all the directions, so faith must
be your map. Never try to make yourself feel
better by finding fault in others. Don't be
misery's company.
Be Blessed!

Day 158

Your life is what you make it. Never blame others for your lack of achievement. Anything worth having is worth the hard work and persistence that is required to obtain it. When rewards come easily, you don't appreciate them. Struggles prepare you for the best that is yet to come.

Be Blessed!

Day 159

Prayer changes things. Anything you want or need to happen can take place as long as you ask God and walk by faith. You are what you think, and you live what you believe.
Be Blessed!

Day 160

Maximize your potential by taking time to get to know yourself. No two people are the same. Your goals and dreams should be as unique as your fingerprint. When you climb out of your own little box, then you will be able to step into reality. The world is smaller than you think.

Be Blessed!

Day 161

Close your eyes, and picture yourself where you desire to be in life. Never limit any dreams you have due to current situations. Any place you go physically, you must first go mentally. Start taking steps toward being the person you've always imagined. No one can trust you until you can first trust yourself.
Be Blessed!

Day 162

We all have areas in our lives that need a little spring cleaning. Mentally and physically get rid of the extra things, thoughts, and people that are taking up valuable space. Make room for the blessings that are coming your way.
Be Blessed!

Day 163

There are many things in life that will bother you, but are you doing anything about them? Complaints are irrelevant; actions are required. Are you a thermometer or a thermostat? Will you keep letting the temperature rise, or are you going to control it?
Be Blessed!

Day 164

The customs of this world shouldn't always be followed. Use caution when making decisions that contradict sound morals. Look at the bigger picture.
Be Blessed!

Day 165

The well-educated and highly skilled aren't always the most successful. Apply your best effort to everything you do. Pay attention when interacting with others.
Be Blessed!

Day 166

We are put on this earth to coexist. Work with others to achieve mutual goals. A lack of teamwork leaves one vulnerable.
Maintain compassion.
Be Blessed!

Day 167

When you take time to get to know Jesus, He will reveal to you the person you truly are. Allow Him to come into your heart and shed light in the dark places that are too deep for you to acknowledge on your own. He knows everything about you. See how authentic He is.

Be Blessed!

Day 168

Settling for less should never be an option. Allow your thoughts to lead you to your destiny. Question anyone that makes you feel less than your true worth. Embrace your power.
Be Blessed!

Day 169

The company you keep can be a stumbling block or a stepping-stone. It's time to jump ship if your crowd isn't heading in the right direction. Hold on to your life raft until it takes you to safe harbor. Use wisdom when considering friends.

Be Blessed!

Day 170

The blind can only lead the blind into a ditch from which they can't help each other escape. Get your house in order. You will be held accountable for you actions. Surround yourself with positive people.
Be Blessed!

Day 171

Move out of your comfort zone. It's time to shake things up. Add some spice to your life so that regrets don't haunt you later. The world is yours. Why not take advantage of it?
Be Blessed!

Day 172

Lights, camera, action! It's time for the blockbuster event of the year: *you!* Make your way to the big screen of life by moving past the things that happened in the past. Start fresh today. Use your story to help others who may be in situations you've overcome. Freely we receive, so freely we should give.

Be Blessed!

Day 173

It doesn't matter what others may say or do—you must want and demand better for yourself. Never blame God for misfortunes in your life. We've all made choices that have instigated the outcomes we've experienced.

Want better, and do better!

Be Blessed!

Day 174

Where you currently are in life is a direct representation of the choices you've made. If you aren't happy with your position, change your direction. There is no way to get a different outcome if your behaviors remain the same. If you don't succeed, it's no one's fault but yours. How bad do you want it?
Be Blessed!

Day 175

When you work hard to obtain your desires, you appreciate them more. The struggle is finding what builds strength and humility. No matter what your expectations are, others can't do your part. Start clearing your path in life. If you can mentally see where you want to be, you will inevitably reach that destination physically if you believe.

Be Blessed!

Day 176

Have you ever wished you could start your life over again? The resolution to your dilemma is Jesus! If you allow Him into your life, the frustrating shell you inhabit will start to peel away like layers to an onion. You will begin to see unnecessary people and routines that dominate your time fade away. Think about it. Be Blessed!

Day 177

When it's over, it's over: *Let it go!* Far too many times, we try to make something out of nothing. Listen to reality when it's speaking to you! Don't live in a fantasy world. Allow God to lead you in your intended direction.
Be Blessed!

Day 178

When you know where you have come from,
you will have a better idea of where you're
going. Validation comes from within. Don't
appraise yourself by the standards of others.
Be Blessed!

Day 179

Sometimes you don't receive your desires because your destiny is greater than your desires. Walk into your season. Discipline separates wishes from reality.
Be Blessed!

Day 180

In order to grow, change is required. If you are doing the same things you did years ago, you're not allowing yourself to get better. Get out of your comfort zone. Failure is a form of redirection. Never give up.
Be Blessed!

Day 181

Birds of a feather flock together. Many people don't have an identity because they choose to be like everyone else. If you follow the crowd, you'll eventually get lost in it. Separate yourself so that you can reach your full potential.

Be Blessed!

Day 182

Get your priorities in order. Learn to accept the things you can't change, and change what you can. You're only able to gain as much as you're willing to lose.
Be Blessed!

Day 183

Having a personal relationship with Jesus Christ is freeing. His love is unconditional. Don't run from peace to entertain pain. Be Blessed!

Day 184

Your existence is measured. Make the most of every moment you possess. The more you invest in your days, the more fulfilled your life will be.

Be Blessed!

Day 185

Everything you do in life is a choice that is made consciously or subconsciously. We tend to blame others for the effects of what we have chosen to do. Take responsibility, and make the necessary adjustments to achieve your goals and live in your purpose. Failure to plan is planning to fail.

Be Blessed!

Day 186

Storms may come from every direction in your life, but you *must* stand strong and hold on. Jesus is a strong and mighty foundation when all else is sinking sand. Never let your problems deal with you. Be proactive in your choices. You only live once.

Be Blessed!

Day 187

Keep your eyes on the prize. Never allow what you're going through or where you are in life to stop you from where you're going. You have the power to change your future by not focusing on your past. Today is a new day. Be Blessed!

Day 188

Life's too short to live a lie! Be honest with
yourself about whom you are and what you
need to improve. Open your mind, and never
judge others. We were made unique so that we
can complement each other's individuality.
Be Blessed!

Day 189

Our ancestors died for our freedom, so *never* take it for granted. Live your life to the fullest. Others laid down their lives to offer you the opportunities you possess. The harder you try to improve your life, the better the quality of your life.
Be Blessed!

Day 190

The obstacles that you are facing now may be related to your surroundings. You are directly and indirectly affected by the problems of those around you. It's always nice to help others, but you can't help those that refuse to help themselves.

Be Blessed!

Day 191

We would like to be in control of every area of our lives, but we're not. You must deal with the issues you can control and give the rest to the Lord. Peace brings about happiness. Let go of the chaos.

Be Blessed!

Day 192

When you need an escape route, and when your enemies have surrounded you, call on your Creator, and you *will* be saved! It doesn't matter who you are or what you've done: He loves you and will protect you. Just open your heart and mind to believe.

Be Blessed!

Day 193

All people should surround themselves with peers who push them to pursue their dreams. No problem in life is too big to be resolved. When the doors of life start to close, faith opens windows for escape.

Be Blessed!

Day 194

When you live life with selfish ambitions, there's no reward at the end of the race. Don't live your life in vain. Sacrifice permits room for receiving. You may have it bad, but someone else has it worse!
Be Blessed!

Day 195

When you tolerate a situation that limits you from being yourself, you are actually sinking, not swimming. Life comes at you like a hurricane, so you must be able to weather the storm! Experience the pain in order to enjoy true joy.
Be Blessed!

Day 196

When things aren't falling into place for you and everyday living is getting too hard to bear, reevaluate your direction. There are always signs along the way that guide you to your intended destination. Stop trying to make your own map.

Be Blessed!

Day 197

Play to win. Put your negative thoughts aside, and reach for the stars. You are not what you're going through. You are more precious than diamonds and gold. How will the world see your beauty if you're not willing to let it shine?

Be Blessed!

Day 198

The circumstances you're faced with are a product of the decisions you've made. Blaming others is a distraction from improving yourself. Learn from your past so that you can live an informed future.
Be Blessed!

Day 199

If you desire change, you must first institute change. You need to surround yourself with people and atmospheres that are sensitive to you and your unique abilities. It is vital for those in your life to assist you in bringing out the best in you and encourage you to aim high! If they're pessimistic, show them the door.
Be Blessed!

Day 200

Be motivated to be optimistic, and possess a reluctance for negativity; it's only poison that pollutes your mind and filters into your life and into the lives of others. Worry quickly leads you astray. Make up your mind that you will be productive.
Be Blessed!

Day 201

If you were going on a road trip, would you leave town without any directions? Why do we go through life without using our instruction manual—the Bible—to lead the way? Understanding isn't always intellectual.
Be Blessed!

Day 202

It's better not to believe in anything than to
be double minded and believe in everything.
Anger and hatred destroy people from the
inside out. Willingly release all negative
thoughts and feelings.
Be Blessed!

Day 203

The world is yours. People who don't care about anything are essentially saying they don't love themselves. You can always tell how people feel about themselves by how they treat others. You can't be honest with others when you lie to yourself.

Be Blessed!

Day 204

Fear is the biggest obstacle to becoming successful. Many worry about the "what ifs" in life instead of pressing forward no matter what the costs. You have to sacrifice in order for you to gain. Where there is joy, there is pain.
Be Blessed!

Day 205

Get the most out of life today! Start claiming everything your heart desires, and watch those things manifest in your life. God can do all things except fail!
Be Blessed!

Day 206

When your back is against the wall, and all you can do is come out swinging, that's when you'll find your true strength. Right now you may think that all is lost, but God's about to restore all that you lost and bless you with increase. All you're required to do is believe that He loves you and is able to restore you. Be Blessed!

Day 207

Don't give up on yourself. The road of life will get rough and danger and dilemmas will come from every direction, but you must be anchored to keep your ship from sinking. By no means should you let the tribulations you currently face dictate who you are. The way you cope with your troubles determines your level of promotion.

Be Blessed!

Day 208

When problems in your life aren't dealt
with, they take over your life like an awful
disease that spreads and kills. The fear of
confrontation can very well be your demise!
Speak when necessary.
Be Blessed!

Day 209

Take things in life for what they are and not what they may seem to be. Focus on solving problems. Being overly sensitive can be a hindrance. Be optimistic but not naïve.
Be Blessed!

Day 210

We should critique ourselves before judging others. If you don't like your current circumstance, change it! You can't control anyone but yourself.
Be Blessed!

Day 211

Don't expect others to handle your business for you. Pity parties only satisfy those who have them. When seeking success, your attitude makes the difference.
Be Blessed!

Day 212

Your time is precious, so make the most of it.
Do the right thing when no one is looking
because eyes are always watching. We all reap
what we sow.
Be Blessed!

Day 213

In God we trust—not in people or their promises. We all coexist. Being selfish could potentially be lethal. Be honest, and think before you speak. When no one is looking, still do the right thing!

Be Blessed!

Day 214

Justification isn't validation. Never allow your selfish ambitions and thoughtless actions to ruin your life. It's never too late to change, but with every breath, time moves on.
Be Blessed!

Day 215

Make the most of your time, and plan for
blessings to come. Now may be the time to
change attitudes, surroundings, or careers.
Success or failure is your choice.
Be Blessed!

Day 216

Deal with problems before they consume you. It's not always about you and how you feel. You must take into consideration the circumstances of others. Selfishness is crippling.
Be Blessed!

Day 217

Constant perseverance brings endless success.
Adopt a new and improved self-image, and let
your imagination take you higher. Don't look
left or right; just focus on the prize ahead.
Be Blessed!

Day 218

Don't dish out anything you can't take in. Evaluate life and circumstances from a different point of view. Be mindful of selfishness because it's not always about you. Be Blessed!

Day 219

Gratitude is a mind-set that must be adopted. Times may be tough, but it could be much worse. Respect both the rain and sunshine because both are needed for life to grow. Be Blessed!

Day 220

Life doesn't always go as planned, but it must go on! Embrace your strengths, and work on your weaknesses. The only way to fail is to give up.
Be Blessed!

Day 221

Before you get wrapped up in what you do or do not receive, remember the reason for the seasons. The pleasures of life are simple; we complicate our existence.

Be Blessed!

Day 222

Things are never as bad as they seem. Take the lemons that life throws at you, and make lemonade. Keep *faith!* Your happiness is worth fighting for.
Be Blessed!

Day 223

Be honest with God about how you feel, for
He cares for you. Don't talk about others
when you haven't figured your situation out.
Honesty with yourself opens the door for
fulfillment.
Be Blessed!

Day 224

Be led where you need to go! Don't try to navigate your route because you will get lost. We make plans, but God sets the final destination.
Be Blessed!

Day 225

Living life answers our questions. Many times reality is in our face, but we are too blind to see it. Appreciate the water before the well runs dry.

Be Blessed!

Day 226

We all face adversity at different times in our lives. How you overcome adversity is as unique as your problem. It won't be easy, but keep seeking, and you shall find.
Be Blessed!

Day 227

Don't look for others to love you more than you love yourself. We all have insecurities and voids that need to be filled. Jesus is the only way to receive true peace.
Be Blessed!

Day 228

If you start out on the top, the only thing you can do is dig a hole for yourself. Work your way up by growing and learning. Trust in the Lord. He will be your foundation.
Be Blessed!

Day 229

Think before you react. Understand that what you say *is* important, but how you say it determines how it is received. Effective communication is the key.
Be Blessed!

Day 230

The situation you've found yourself in isn't your permanent location. Make changes that positively affect your life and the lives of others.
Be Blessed!

Day 231

Your struggle encourages others through their pain. You won't always see the big picture; instead, you view life one scene at a time. The opposition that pursues you will ultimately pay off.

Be Blessed!

Day 232

Be a sponge in the lives of others. Allow the Holy Spirit to saturate you and squeeze your blessings out onto the world. The presence of the Lord isn't for you to keep inside under lock and key. Don't judge others; instead, spread your love to the masses.

Be Blessed!

Day 233

Even in your darkest hour, you aren't alone. No matter how distant help and refuge may seem, you were created to succeed. Pray for optimism and patience. The best is yet to come when you anticipate great things. Be Blessed!

Day 234

Allow opposition to be ammunition for your achievement. Beat your enemy at his own game; you can't fight fire with fuel. Think smart and thoroughly. The road ahead will prove you to be victorious.

Be Blessed!

Day 235

Folks may seem to have your best interests in mind, but you should dig a little deeper. Be mindful of the motives of those around you. Don't leave your heart out to be broken.
Be Blessed!

Day 236

There are times in life when you must catapult yourself to the next level. Live life day by day, planning for the future but not obsessing over what's unknown. Remember that your life is what you make of it.

Be Blessed!

Day 237

Make yourself available to those who desire to invest in your purpose. Pray for discernment that allows you to differentiate those who are authentic from those who are counterfeit. If your blessing were staring you in your face, would you recognize them?

Be Blessed!

Day 238

A time will come when ultimatums must be enforced. Sometimes a situation must completely die in order for new life to begin. Take an assessment of where you are and whom you are with. Determine what needs to carry on and what needs to come to an end. Be Blessed!

Day 239

Love gets better and deeper with attention and time. The love you bestow upon others must never exceed the affection and care you award to yourself. Uncover the mysteries within. The more you understand yourself, the more your dealings with others will improve.

Be Blessed!

Day 240

Oftentimes the situations that cause the most pain in life bring about the most joy. Learn to embrace who you are and what you've been through. Your darkest hours will shed light on the lives of those who feel hopeless and insufficient. A *test* always precedes a *test*imony. Be Blessed!

Day 241

Be adamant about having mentors in your
life who have your best interests in mind.
There will be many wolves in sheep's clothing,
but you are expected to dodge their attacks.
Discernment, humility, and honesty will take
you places where riches and fame fall short.
Be Blessed!

Day 242

Pride causes a false sense of security. Blessings are often disguised in tests of character that try your faith. React after thinking things through.
Be Blessed!

Day 243

Sing a song; tell a story; do a dance that communicates your unique personality and challenges others to do the same. This world is a melting pot of beauty due to the differences that we each possess. Accept your individuality; there you will find familiarity. Be Blessed!

Day 244

Allow the wonder of miracles to enter your life
through optimism. Life is rough. Times get
hard. But God can't fail! Welcome Him into
your world, and He will give you peace
of mind.
Be Blessed!

Day 245

Though there will be issues in life,
remember that troubles don't last always.
Just as the seasons change, so do your life's
circumstances. Patience and perseverance are
vital for a pristine way of life.
Be Blessed!

Day 246

Peace is a vital necessity to healthy living.
Life's uncertainties often cause anxious
feelings. Worrying can't fix a situation, but
faith brings about change.
Be Blessed!

Day 247

You'll never get ahead if you keep looking back. Nasty things may have happened in your past, but that was to prepare and mold you into the successful person you are destined to be. Use hope and faith as ammunition to reach for the sky.
Be Blessed!

Day 248

Be patient, and build upon what you have; don't tear it down. Temptation can distract you from what's important. Don't make permanent decisions from temporary circumstances. Commit to the matters of your heart that are most important.
Be Blessed!

Day 249

Communication is vital in every relationship. Let people know how you feel and where you're coming from. The truth will set you and others free.
Be Blessed!

Day 250

When you've done all you can do, sometimes you have to walk away and let it go. Others may be reluctant to leave. Complement who you are by being true to yourself. No one can love you until you love yourself.

Be Blessed!

Day 251

Be mindful of constructive criticism.
Decisions must be given thought, but too
much pondering can prove to be confusing.
You will never know until you try.
Be Blessed!

Day 252

When someone truly cares, his or her actions speak louder than words. Explore new ways to express how you feel. Silence often speaks loudly. Everyone has a language of love; find yours.

Be Blessed!

Day 253

Give God the glory! It's not about being fake or "holier than thou"; it's about acknowledging who *truly* loves you and controls your destiny. Jesus died so that you may have an escape route from self-destruction. Giving praise in your own special way is the least you can do. Be Blessed!

Day 254

Reason and logic can't accurately decipher the next road you should take in life. Sometimes the best ideas don't make sense. Faith can lead you to peace and prosperity for the rest of your days. Step out of the box.
Be Blessed!

Day 255

Arrogance is a mask for jealousy and insecurity. Don't bring others down because it hurts too much to deal with your problems. What goes around comes around. Be ready to receive whatever you dish out.

Be Blessed!

Day 256

Dance to a new tune, and beat a new drum!
Take the fresh new ideas that flow within
you, and put them into action. Life has many
uncertainties, but you can count on faith to
bring you through. Fear says, "You're OK
where you are; other people have it worse,"
but faith says, "I can make it to where I desire
to go and reach back down to help those who
yearn to advance also."
Be Blessed!

Day 257

Biting the hand that feeds you is dangerous in many ways. Don't give your resources more respect than your primary source. Be honest and faithful to what is true. Embrace the tests that await you; they are preparing you for the blessings to come.

Be Blessed!

Day 258

It is better to be honest with little than deceitful with much. Don't value your life by the standards of others. Rest assured that no bad deed goes unpunished.
Be Blessed!

Day 259

Customs, ideas, and habits are roadblocks preventing you from getting ahead. You must try new things, and you must let go of the past in order to prosper in the future.
Be Blessed!

Day 260

When the end is near, that is evidence of a new beginning. Time heals wounds that are allowed to heal. Learn from your mistakes, and keep pressing on. It's your season.
Be Blessed!

Day 261

It's hard to be patient when the walls are tumbling down, but worrying won't change any situation. Be optimistic. The best is yet to come.

Be Blessed!

Day 262

Take time to evaluate the situation before jumping to conclusions. Be open to different points of view. Your character is tested by your responses to adversity.

Be Blessed!

Day 263

Exhibit patience by waiting with an optimistic
attitude. Time passes minute by minute.
You must decide if it passes by pleasantly.
Worrying worsens your quality of life.
Be Blessed!

Day 264

You are a product of what you focus your time and attention on. We like to blame others for our downfalls, but we make the choices that bring about success or failure. Stop feeling sorry for yourself. We should learn from the past—*forgive* but never *forget*—so that we don't make the same mistakes twice. Be Blessed!

Day 265

Even if you're a teacher, you will always be a student. Those who know everything can't be taught anything. Take time to absorb information that can enhance your quality of life.
Be Blessed!

Day 266

Age doesn't matter; you're never too old to learn. Commit to being a great student in the school of life; being a student will teach you everything you need to learn.
Be Blessed!

Day 267

Patience is vital but hard to attain. Keep your
eyes and your heart open to see and receive
the blessings that are to come. Step out
in faith.
Be Blessed!

Day 268

Forgiveness allows for regeneration of the self. Resentment occupies valuable mental space. Let go of hindrances, and embrace available help.
Be Blessed!

Day 269

We must be open to people in our lives that have honest and sobering advice, comments, and opinions. No one knows the answer to everything. Having healthy relationships with others allows us to give and receive valuable information.

Be Blessed!

Day 270

Make a joyful noise! This day is what you make of it. Time waits on no one. You may not be able to get back what you've lost. Make the most out of every situation.
Be Blessed!

Day 271

Plant many seeds when preparing for a great harvest. Don't put all of your eggs in one basket. Life doesn't always go as planned! Be Blessed!

Day 272

Feelings may influence how you act or react, but they aren't always accurate. Being misinformed can cause your perspective to be out of focus. Any action you take may be justified, but that does not make it right. Be Blessed!

Day 273

Accountability is necessary to keep you on track. No matter the issue, others don't determine your livelihood. Work hard to improve yourself. Despise pity and pity parties.
Be Blessed!

Day 274

Establish boundaries, and maintain your ground. You can't expect others to respect your space if they don't know where you stand. Speak up, and take your position. Be Blessed!

Day 275

Even strong young lions sometimes go hungry, but those who trust in the Lord will never lack any good thing (Ps 34:10). You may not get everything you want, but you will possess all that you need. Be grateful and appreciative. Your life really could have been so much worse.
Be Blessed!

Day 276

Now faith is the substance of things hoped for, the evidence of things not seen (Hebrews 11:1). Keep faith in your vision, and you will find yourself wherever you've imagined. No vision means no happiness, and no fulfillment means no joy. You can do all things through Christ who strengthens you.
Be Blessed!

Day 277

There is an amazing grace awaiting your soul. Allow your peace to flow like a river. Don't let the limitations of others hold you hostage.
Be Blessed!

Day 278

Not everyone is privileged with choices.
Be thankful for options, and take advantage
of them. Don't take for granted your potential
to succeed.
Be Blessed!

Day 279

Faith is the evidence of what you can't see.
When you have problems, your beliefs will
see you through. Your burdens aren't yours to
carry. Cast your cares on the Lord.
Be Blessed!

Day 280

When you are drowning in your own grief, pain, and insecurities, there is a secure lifeline. Giving up is not an option. Instead, give life all that you have.
Be Blessed!

Day 281

You won't know if you like something unless you try it. Judging a book by its cover is deceiving and costly. Step out in faith, and try new things.
Be Blessed!

Day 282

Do you know who you are, or are you playing life like it's a game? True purpose and worth will never be found in the mind or hands of humans. Purpose is realized by divine intuition. Looking around to find who you should be will leave you walking in circles. Be Blessed!

Day 283

Unless you walk by faith, pressing circumstances will always cloud your vision. To truly follow the right path, your faith must neutralize your fears. Holding on to the past means you're letting go of your future.
Be Blessed!

Day 284

Finding who you are comes from looking within, not from looking around. What works for others isn't necessarily what you were called to do. Think outside of the box.
Be Blessed!

Day 285

Negative thoughts are like poisons that contaminate your life. Feelings and perceptions are often incorrect. You are what you believe. Faith is patience and belief in God and His word.

Be Blessed!

Day 286

Free your mind to unlock freedom in your life. Whatever the problem, faith and honesty will present a solution. Call yourself who you want to be, not who you see now.
Be Blessed!

Day 287

The blessing God has for you already has your name on it! It's your season to live what you've been praying for. Belief precedes receiving. Be Blessed!

Day 288

The fear of the Lord brings peace and prosperity. The more you wander away from Him, the deeper you dig your own pit. Prayer changes things.
Be Blessed!

Day 289

Your feelings and perceptions may cloud your awareness of the truth. Ask questions and seek knowledge so that you won't come up short.
Never assume.
Be Blessed!

Day 290

We all experience good and bad times. Don't allow negativity to weigh you down. Life is about living through the sunshine and the rain. Learn from your experiences.
Be Blessed!

Day 291

Whether you believe it or not, heaven and hell are real. Changing your life isn't about giving up fun; it's about changing the *way* you have fun. You have never done anything that blocks you from the grace of God! Faith is what changes you—faith that you don't have to continue being who you were before.
Be Blessed!

Day 292

Your mind—the way you think—can be your best friend or worst enemy. Condition your thought process so that you can always strive for improvement. You are what you think. Be Blessed!

Day 293

Every step you make is an improvement from the one before. Whether you are going forward or backward, you're learning in the process. Embrace every lesson learned, whether it is pleasant or difficult. Every circumstance has a specific purpose.
Be Blessed!

Day 294

There is nothing you can do to deserve God's grace. It's a *gift!* His love is given freely, so freely we should receive it. Make improvements a step at a time.
Be Blessed!

Day 295

Love is such a powerful force. Someone you love can be long gone, but his or her spirit and accompanying memories live on. Whether they are no longer here or the season in which they were sent to your life has ended, you can't get away from true love. From the highest mountain to the deepest sea, love chases you, so you wait and see. I knew love and still do; no matter where I am, it's with me too.

God *is* love.

Be Blessed!

Day 296

Do what you need to do, not just what you want. Strive for excellence, even if others are content with being average. Live your life without limits.
Be Blessed!

Day 297

Be thankful for every day. God always makes a way. You may stumble and fall, but you will get back up. Only God can truly judge, but healthy criticism is invaluable. The fear of rejection could be your demise.

Be Blessed!

Day 298

Trials and troubles come so that we may be a lamp to others walking down the dark path behind us. It's easier to help someone through a situation that you have overcome. Wisdom should be shared and not hoarded or used in judgment. Share your insight. Your testimony has saving power.

Be Blessed!

Day 299

Wisdom brings about prosperity. You can't do it all on your own. One can move one thousand, but two can move ten thousand. Allow the right players to join your team. Be Blessed!

Day 300

Pick your battles. Don't sweat the little things.
God is always in control. Doing your best is
all that you're required to do.
Be Blessed!

Day 301

Why do some people judge and condemn others while their situations stink? It's funny how people run from their blessings instead of embracing them. Hitting rock bottom may hurt, but staying there can be your demise. Material things are just material. Invest in treasures that won't rust and rot.

Be Blessed!

Day 302

The Lord helps the fallen and lifts those bent beneath their loads. Life is hard, but you have a Savior to lean on. Don't try to do it all by yourself.
Be Blessed!

Day 303

Allow your wounds to heal; don't live in the past. Embrace the present while anticipating your future. Where you invest your time and money is where you'll get your return.

Be Blessed!

Day 304

It's funny how those who put in little effort often expect a great return. Your intentions aren't always evident in your actions. Be genuine in your dealings.
Be Blessed!

Day 305

Faith is believing and then seeing. Hope is expecting something that doesn't even make sense. Whatever you insist on having will persist. Make the decision to believe.
Be Blessed!

Day 306

Make room for increase in your life. Get rid of outdated attitudes and mind-sets. Your expectations must align with your desires. Be Blessed!

Day 307

Materialism is a sickness that afflicts many people. Tell me the last time you saw a moving truck back up at a gravesite or a casket full of designer clothes and shoes. Life is too short to be consumed with treasures that have no lasting value. We all like nice things, but having them shouldn't consume you. Is your heart right?
Be Blessed!

Day 308

We often say that if someone in our lives would only do *this* or if they had done *that*, things would be so much easier. It's funny how we expect others to do right by us but don't always return the sentiments. Before you get upset with others about their faults, make sure you have addressed your own.

Be Blessed!

Day 309

Seeking revenge is worrisome. Turning the other cheek is an indication of strength, not a sign of weakness. Those who hurt you are slowly and steadily afflicting themselves.
Be Blessed!

Day 310

After comparisons have been made, and after blames have been directed, you must still make an honest effort to improve. Be accountable.
Be Blessed!

Day 311

Sometimes bad things happen so that you can appreciate the good things in your life. Don't be so focused on the destination that your neglect to enjoy the journey!
Be Blessed!

Day 312

To live and not love truly isn't living. Tests and trials come to make you stronger, not tear you apart. Cherish those who are close to you, and show them that you care.

Be Blessed!

Day 313

Before you figure out the solution, you must first identify the problem. Constructive criticism makes room for growth. Don't take correction personally.

Be Blessed!

Day 314

Change is impossible to escape. The most potent pills that life administers are usually the hardest to swallow. Whether or not we're fond of the taste, facing reality is the best medicine. Seek peace and wisdom; they will set you free.

Be Blessed!

Day 315

The giants in your life aren't as big as they seem. Your thought process is your biggest enemy. Have faith, and ask God to give you the correct perspective.

Be Blessed!

Day 316

Take an inventory of your life. Attitudes, people, and situations may be taking up valuable space. Make room for peace and changes to breakthrough. Release the burdens of setbacks. You can't receive increase if there is no room to grow.

Be Blessed!

Day 317

In your darkest hours, you can shed light into the lives of others. Learn from your wrong turns; you will then be able to give directions to those who are lost. Don't discredit your experience.
Be Blessed!

Day 318

We must be strategic in how we reach out to others. Let's not get too wrapped up in our own personal desires that we forget to help those who have fallen and don't know how to get up. Many people possess a careless attitude because they don't know *how* to care.

Be Blessed!

Day 319

Writing down your thoughts, feelings, dreams, and desires is a blueprint to your life. You can't strictly operate through emotion. Planning is necessary. The end reward is peace, transparency, and success.
Be Blessed!

Day 320

You can make plans, but the Lord orders your steps. Expectations often seem impossible. Discipline removes the boundaries of impossibilities.
Be Blessed!

Day 321

God is awesome! He tries our hearts through tests and trials. He comforts us through pain and leads us through storms. Jesus accomplished more on the cross than we will ever know. When we put our trust in Him, we will become *more* than conquerors.

Be Blessed!

Day 322

Fear and anxiety can alter your judgment.
View the joys and pains of life through a lens
of expectation. Look past your troubles so that
you can make it through.
Be Blessed!

Day 323

We will never know the time or the hour when we will leave this place called earth. Let's hold on to love and release malice, stress, and worry. Life is too short and unpredictable to waste time on foolishness. If you are offended, *speak up*. Don't take people and their actions personally.

Be Blessed!

Day 324

Your surroundings don't dictate your identity.
Learn from your mistakes to avoid repeating
them. Leave your past behind, and walk
into your future. Similarities don't make
us the same.
Be Blessed!

Day 325

Be grateful, regardless of your circumstances.
Times may be rough, but there is always
someone who has it worse. Be grateful for the
good, and learn from the bad.
Be Blessed!

Day 326

The trials you experience today will be triumphs tomorrow. Keep trying; good deeds are never done in vain. Don't give up.
Be Blessed!

Day 327

There are some people and situations you will never understand. Find the purpose in every interaction. Even in confusion, there is always some clarity.

Be Blessed!

Day 328

Face your fears, or they will overtake
you. Confrontation doesn't have to be
uncomfortable, but it is often necessary.
Conquer the beast of fear.
Be Blessed!

Day 329

Smooth words hide deceitful hearts. Things aren't always what they present themselves to be. Be careful that the mouths you feed don't turn and bite you.
Be Blessed!

Day 330

Life throws unexpected pitches that may cause you to strike out. Keep batting until you hit that home run. Persistence is the ingredient to success.
Be Blessed!

Day 331

Wisdom is the key to understanding different situations. Some things don't need to be understood, let alone tolerated. People and circumstances have cunning ways of expressing their true intentions—whether negative or positive. Learn from every situation—even how *not* to do things.
Be Blessed!

Day 332

Some things in life don't make sense, and they never will. Why do we waste time trying to figure foolishness out? Time is precious and priceless and should be used wisely. Avoid procrastination whenever possible. Think outside of the box.
Be Blessed!

Day 333

Charm is deceptive, and our emotions sometimes lie. Seek an awareness of reality instead of the mirage created by feelings. Understand that an opposing opinion isn't necessarily incorrect.

Be Blessed!

Day 334

You don't fall in and out of true love. The way you love may change, but the substance is still there. Let go of resentment and anger so that you can *move on!*
Be Blessed!

Day 335

Everyone who presents a need isn't necessarily needy. Use wisdom and discernment when dealing with others. Kindness shouldn't be a weakness. Beware of deceit.
Be Blessed!

Day 336

Your perception of who you are determines where you go in life. Aim high, and dream big. You are bound to face problems, but remember that there is always a solution. Be Blessed!

Day 337

Sometimes you must take a loss in order to gain. Be patient, and weigh your options. The future is never clear. Prosperity is inevitable to those who have faith.

Be Blessed!

Day 338

It is amazing how some people can be an inspiration even when they are feeling down themselves. Keep hope, and have faith that everything will work out. Life is too short to hate on others. Strive to be a blessing, and you will be blessed in the process.

Be Blessed!

Day 339

Life often prescribes tough pills to swallow; though we don't like them, they are good for us and make us better. We sometimes cling to people, situations, mind-sets, and attitudes that never complemented our purpose. Free yourself from the burdens that make you sick. Be Blessed!

Day 340

Storms in life come to test your durability and destroy attitudes that hinder your growth. Embrace the rain as well as the sunshine. Be Blessed!

Day 341

Knowing what you need to do is half of your battle, but doing it is a war in itself. Swallow your pride; it leads to disgrace. There is nothing worse than being so wise that you make yourself foolish.
Be Blessed!

Day 342

Keep pressing on, no matter what the forecast may be. Faith can turn a storm into a warm and sunny day. Optimism is the key to unlocking your destiny.
Be Blessed!

Day 343

Let's give the gift that keeps on giving: love. Life is too short to hold grudges in your heart. Deal with any problems and issues immediately, and move on. Holding on to malice only hinders your growth. His anger lasts for a moment, but His favor lasts for a lifetime. Weeping may endure for a night, but joy comes in the morning (Ps 30:5).

Be Blessed!

Day 344

Your enemies have no power over you that you haven't allowed them to have. Never give up on your dreams. Other people's opinions may be useful but are not the guidelines that you must follow.
Be Blessed!

Day 345

Many people are trying to be something or someone they aren't. You have a specific purpose on this planet, and even though someone else's job may look more glamorous and enjoyable, it doesn't mean you need to change your focus. Being an individual allows you to work effectively and collectively with others without losing yourself. Everything that glitters is *not* gold.

Be Blessed!

Day 346

Faith sustains life. When your back is against the wall, faith is an escape route. Stays focused on your vision, and keep planting seeds. Eventually, all of your labor will produce a great harvest.
Be Blessed!

Day 347

Give the gift that keeps on giving. Love, and be loved. It enhances your quality of life. Stress and anger are silent killers with lasting effects.

Be Blessed!

Day 348

Don't play with other people's feelings.
Though no one may be looking, it doesn't
mean you're not seen. Long-term losses will
outweigh short-term benefits. Weigh your
options.
Be Blessed!

Day 349

Your thoughts directly relate to your actions.
Be optimistic, no matter what the forecast
says. Time heals all wounds. Take advantage
of all opportunities.
Be Blessed!

Day 350

Pursuing happiness can rob you of enjoying life. Learn from your successes and mistakes. New beginnings must first take place in your mind.
Be Blessed!

Day 351

Give an ear to wisdom. Doses of reality won't always taste good, but they will help you along the journey of life. Endure the hardships, and you will enjoy the rewards.

Be Blessed!

Day 352

The right decision isn't always the easiest.
Make choices with your future in mind;
today's trouble is tomorrow's past. Don't lose
your destiny to fear.
Be Blessed!

Day 353

Sometimes you must follow your heart and press pause on reality. Life is too short; we should all live to the fullest with no regrets. Sometimes actions that don't line up with reason fall in line with your destiny.
Be Blessed!

Day 354

Your deepest sacrifice will bring about your greatest reward. Keep trying; the best is yet to come. Check your attitude. You can't take everyone with you.
Be Blessed!

Day 355

Giving it your all shouldn't deplete you; it should enhance your character. Look at the big picture and not just at one scene at a time. Finish whatever you start.
Be Blessed!

Day 356

Think about yourself when interacting with others. No good or bad deed goes unnoticed. Karma is real. Be careful when sowing seeds. Be Blessed!

Day 357

Loyalty supersedes flattery. Give loved ones their compliments and flowers while they can hear and smell them. You'll never know when the last day is near.

Be Blessed!

Day 358

Life is a constant battle of the fittest. It takes faith to truly reach out and touch where your dreams are leading you. Your efforts signify how badly you want to succeed. You never know how strong you are until your strength is tested.
Be Blessed!

Day 359

Sowing seeds of patience will bear much fruit in your life. Your perception of a matter decides the benefits you will receive. Closed minds won't allow ideas in or out. Be creative when getting your point across.

Be Blessed!

Day 360

The pitfalls in life clear the way for comebacks. Appreciate the lessons learned, and use them to navigate your journey. Don't let the past steal your future.
Be Blessed!

Day 361

Hard decisions are often the most liberating. Plan on success; failure is not an option. You are either your own best friend or your own worst enemy.

Be Blessed!

Day 362

Be mindful of your perception of those you encounter. Great gifts may come in unassuming packages. Don't lose yourself in accommodating others.
Be Blessed!

Day 363

What worked in the past may not be sufficient for your future. Learn from your triumphs as well as your trials. An ending must take place in order to begin again.
Be Blessed!

Day 364

Persuasion doesn't guarantee change. If your circle only makes withdrawals and no deposits, it may be time to invest elsewhere.
Be Blessed!

Day 365

Sometimes we get so caught up in the pursuit of the destination that we neglect to enjoy the scenery along the way. Some distractions come to expose areas in your life that need more attention. Keep on living, and the things and people that really matter will shine like the sun in your life.

Be Blessed!

Day 366

Don't over analyze the situation. Be quick in your observations, not your assumptions. Learn from your issues. Anger breeds strife. Be Blessed

Day 367

Your *wants* may present themselves as *needs*, but humility makes room for greatness to enter your life. Don't take for granted the opportunities that may escort your dreams into reality. Self-inventory minimizes loss.
Be Blessed!

Made in the USA
Lexington, KY
14 March 2017